Erica,

May you find inspiration in these readings.

Love

Your old Principal

Ms OBrien

GATHERING
PROMISES

GATHERING PROMISES

GATHERING
PROMISES

The Message is a contemporary rendering of the Bible from
the original languages, crafted to present its tone, rhythm,
events, and ideas in everyday speech.

EXTRAVAGANTLY
LOVED

The Father loves the Son extravagantly. He turned everything over to him so he could give it away—a lavish distribution of gifts. That is why whoever accepts and trusts the Son gets in on everything, life complete and forever!

John 3:34-36

PROMISES

Before you know it the Son of Man
will arrive with all the splendor of his
Father, accompanied by an army of angels.
You'll get everything you have coming
to you, a personal gift.

■ ■ ■ ■ ■ ■ ■ ■ ■ ■ ■ ■ ■

Matthew 16:27

P R O M I S E S

He came to his own people,
but they didn't want him.
But whoever did want him,
who believed he was who he claimed
and would do what he said,
He made to be their true selves,
their child-of-God selves.

■ ■ ■ ■ ■ ■ ■ ■ ■ ■ ■ ■ ■

John 1:11-12

PROMISES

It is necessary for the Son of Man to be lifted up—and everyone who looks up to him, trusting and expectant, will gain a real life, eternal life.

This is how much God loved the world: He gave his Son, his one and only Son. And this is why: so that no one need be destroyed; by believing in him, anyone can have a whole and lasting life. God didn't go to all the trouble of sending his Son merely to point an accusing finger, telling the world how bad it was. He came to help, to put the world right again.

■ ■ ■ ■ ■ ■ ■ ■ ■ ■ ■ ■ ■ ■

John 3:14-17

PROMISES

Steep yourself in God-reality, God-initiative, God-provisions. You'll find all your everyday human concerns will be met. Don't be afraid of missing out. You're my dearest friends! The Father wants to give you the very kingdom itself.

■ ■ ■ ■ ■ ■ ■ ■ ■ ■ ■ ■ ■ ■

Luke 12:31-32

PROMISES

$\mathcal{A}$ll you who fear GOD,
how blessed you are!
how happily you walk on his
smooth straight road!...
Enjoy the blessing! Revel in the goodness!...
Oh, how he blesses the one who fears GOD!

■ ■ ■ ■ ■ ■ ■ ■ ■ ■ ■ ■ ■

Psalm 128:1-2,4

PROMISES

Oh my soul, bless GOD,
don't forget a single blessing!
He forgives your sins—every one.
He heals your diseases—every one.
He redeems you from hell—saves your life!
He crowns you with love and mercy—
a paradise crown.
He wraps you in goodness—beauty eternal.
He renews your youth—you're always
young in his presence.

■ ■ ■ ■ ■ ■ ■ ■ ■ ■ ■ ■ ■ ■

Psalm 103:2-5

PROMISES

But if you make yourselves at home with me and my words are at home in you, you can be sure that whatever you ask will be listened to and acted upon....

If you keep my commands, you'll remain intimately at home in my love. That's what I've done—kept my Father's commands and made myself at home in his love.

I've told you these things for a purpose: that my joy might be your joy, and your joy wholly mature.

■ ■ ■ ■ ■ ■ ■ ■ ■ ■ ■ ■ ■

John 15:7, 10-11

PROMISES

This is what I want you to do: Ask the Father for whatever is in keeping with the things I've revealed to you. Ask in my name, according to my will, and he'll most certainly give it to you. Your joy will be a river overflowing its banks!

■ ■ ■ ■ ■ ■ ■ ■ ■ ■ ■ ■ ■ ■

John 16:23

PROMISES

PROMISES

$\mathcal{A}$ woman, a Samaritan, came to draw water. Jesus said, "Would you give me a drink of water?" (His disciples had gone to the village to buy food for lunch.)

The Samaritan woman, taken aback, asked, "How come you, a Jew, are asking me, a Samaritan woman, for a drink?" (Jews in those days wouldn't be caught dead talking to Samaritans.)

PROMISES

Jesus answered, "If you knew the generosity of God and who I am, you would be asking me for a drink, and I would give you fresh, living water."

The woman said, "Sir, you don't even have a bucket to draw with, and this well is deep. So how are you going to get this 'living water'? Are you a better man than our ancestor Jacob, who dug this well and drank from it, he and his sons and livestock, and passed it down to us?"

$\mathcal{J}$esus said, "Everyone who drinks this water will get thirsty again and again. Anyone who drinks the water I give will never thirst—not ever. The water I give will be an artesian spring within, gushing fountains of endless life."

■ ■ ■ ■ ■ ■ ■ ■ ■ ■ ■ ■ ■

John 4:7-14

PROMISES

$\mathcal{O}$ur Savior Jesus poured out new life
so generously. God's gift has restored
our relationship with him and given us
back our lives. And there's more life
to come—an eternity of life!

■ ■ ■ ■ ■ ■ ■ ■ ■ ■ ■ ■ ■ ■

Titus 3:6-7

PROMISES

$\mathcal{J}$ust think—you don't need a thing, you've got it all! All God's gifts are right in front of you as you wait expectantly for our Master Jesus to arrive on the scene for the Finale. And not only that, but God himself is right alongside to keep you steady and on track until things are all wrapped up by Jesus. God, who got you started in this spiritual adventure, shares with us the life of his Son and our Master Jesus. He will never give up on you. Never forget that.

■ ■ ■ ■ ■ ■ ■ ■ ■ ■ ■ ■ ■ ■

1 Corinthians 1:7-9

PROMISES

*H*allelujah!
Praise God in his holy house of worship,
praise him under the open skies;
Praise him for his acts of power,
praise him for his magnificent greatness...
Let every living, breathing
creature praise GOD!
Hallelujah!

■ ■ ■ ■ ■ ■ ■ ■ ■ ■ ■ ■ ■

Psalm 150:1-2,6

PROMISES

GENEROUS
IN GIFTS
AND
GLORY

All sunshine and sovereign is GOD,
generous in gifts and glory.

■ ■ ■ ■ ■ ■ ■ ■ ■ ■ ■ ■ ■ ■

Psalm 84:11

PROMISES

$\mathscr{W}$hat a God we have! And how fortunate we are to have him, this Father of our Master Jesus! Because Jesus was raised from the dead, we've been given a brand-new life and have everything to live for, including a future in heaven—and the future starts now! God is keeping careful watch over us and the future. The Day is coming when you'll have it all—life healed and whole.

▪▪▪▪▪▪▪▪▪▪▪▪▪▪

1 Peter 1:3-5

PROMISES

$\mathcal{G}$OD is sheer mercy and grace;
not easily angered, he's rich in love....
He doesn't treat us as our sins deserve,
nor pay us back in full for our wrongs.

PROMISES

As high as heaven is over the earth,
so strong is his love to those who fear him.
And as far as sunrise is from sunset,
he has separated us from our sins.

■ ■ ■ ■ ■ ■ ■ ■ ■ ■ ■ ■ ■

Psalm 103:8,10-12

$\mathcal{Y}$ou never saw him, yet you love him. You still don't see him, yet you trust him.... Because you kept on believing, you'll get what you're looking forward to: total salvation.

■ ■ ■ ■ ■ ■ ■ ■ ■ ■ ■ ■ ■ ■

1 Peter 1:8-9

PROMISES

*N*ow we look inside, and what we see
is that anyone united with the Messiah gets
a fresh start, is created new. The old life
is gone; a new life burgeons!

■ ■ ■ ■ ■ ■ ■ ■ ■ ■ ■ ■ ■ ■

2 Corinthians 5:17

*N*ow you have arrived at your destination:
By faith in Christ you are in direct
relationship with God.

■ ■ ■ ■ ■ ■ ■ ■ ■ ■ ■ ■ ■ ■

Galatians 3:26

PROMISES

OUR GOD GIVES YOU EVERYTHING YOU NEED, MAKES YOU EVERYTHING YOU'RE TO BE.

2 Thessalonians 1:2

$\mathcal{G}$od's Spirit is right alongside helping us along. If we don't know how or what to pray, it doesn't matter. He does our praying in and for us, making prayer out of our wordless sighs, our aching groans. He knows us far better than we know ourselves, knows our...condition, and keeps us present before God. That's why we can be so sure that every detail in our lives of love for God is worked into something good.

■ ■ ■ ■ ■ ■ ■ ■ ■ ■ ■ ■ ■ ■

Romans 8:26-28

PROMISES

*I*n the Messiah, in Christ, God leads us from place to place in one perpetual victory parade. Through us, he brings knowledge of Christ. Everywhere we go, people breathe in the exquisite fragrance. Because of Christ, we give off a sweet scent rising to God, which is recognized by those on the way of salvation— an aroma redolent with life.

■ ■ ■ ■ ■ ■ ■ ■ ■ ■ ■ ■ ■ ■

2 Corinthians 2:14-15

*H*onor GOD with everything you own;
give him the first and the best.
Your barns will burst,
your wine vats will brim over.

■ ■ ■ ■ ■ ■ ■ ■ ■ ■ ■ ■ ■

Proverbs 3:9-10

PROMISES

Every desirable and beneficial gift comes out of heaven. The gifts are rivers of light cascading down from the Father of Light.

James 1:17

PROMISES

$\mathcal{T}$he payoff for meekness and Fear-of-GOD
is plenty and honor and a satisfying life.

■ ■ ■ ■ ■ ■ ■ ■ ■ ■ ■ ■ ■ ■

Proverbs 22:4

PROMISES

$\mathcal{G}$od, you did everything you promised,
and I'm thanking you with all my heart.
You pulled me from the brink of death,
my feet from the cliff-edge of doom.
Now I stroll at leisure with God
in the sunlit fields of life.

■ ■ ■ ■ ■ ■ ■ ■ ■ ■ ■ ■ ■

Psalm 56:12-13

PROMISES

You can be sure that God will take care of
everything you need, his generosity exceeding
even yours in the glory that pours from Jesus.
Our God and Father abounds in glory
that just pours out into eternity.

■ ■ ■ ■ ■ ■ ■ ■ ■ ■ ■ ■ ■

Philippians 4:19-20

PROMISES

*G*od can do anything, you know—far
more than you could ever imagine or guess or
request in your wildest dreams! He does it not
by pushing us around but by working within us,
his Spirit deeply and gently within us.
Glory to God in the church!
Glory to God in the Messiah, in Jesus!
Glory down all the generations!
Glory through all millennia!

■ ■ ■ ■ ■ ■ ■ ■ ■ ■ ■ ■ ■

Ephesians 3:20-21

PROMISES

SEEK AND
YOU WILL
FIND

$\mathcal{A}$sk and you'll get;
Seek and you'll find;
Knock and the door will open.
Don't bargain with God. Be direct.
Ask for what you need.

■ ■ ■ ■ ■ ■ ■ ■ ■ ■ ■ ■ ■

Luke 11:9-10

PROMISES

I love those who love me;
those who look for me find me.

■ ■ ■ ■ ■ ■ ■ ■ ■ ■ ■ ■ ■

Proverbs 8:17

PROMISES

$\mathcal{F}$riends, when life gets really difficult, don't jump to the conclusion that God isn't on the job. Instead, be glad that you are in the very thick of what Christ experienced. This is a spiritual refining process, with glory just around the corner.

■ ■ ■ ■ ■ ■ ■ ■ ■ ■ ■ ■ ᠈ ■

1 Peter 4:12-13

PROMISES

$\mathcal{G}$OD is fair and just;
He corrects the misdirected,
Sends them in the right direction...
And leads them step by step.
From now on every road you travel
Will take you to GOD.

■ ■ ■ ■ ■ ■ ■ ■ ■ ■ ■ ■ ■

Psalm 25:8-10

PROMISES

Eight days later, his disciples were again in the room. This time Thomas was with them. Jesus came through the locked doors, stood among them, and said, "Peace to you."

Then he focused his attention on Thomas. "Take your finger and examine my hands. Take your hand and stick it in my side. Don't be unbelieving. Believe."

PROMISES

Thomas said, "My Master! My God!"
Jesus said, "So, you believe because you've seen
with your own eyes. Even better blessings are in
store for those who believe without seeing."

■ ■ ■ ■ ■ ■ ■ ■ ■ ■ ■ ■ ■ ■

John 20:26-29

PROMISES

*K*eep your eye on the healthy soul,
scrutinize the straight life;
There's a future
in strenuous wholeness....
The spacious, free life is from GOD,
it's also protected and safe.
GOD-strengthened, we're delivered from evil—
when we run to him, he saves us.

■ ■ ■ ■ ■ ■ ■ ■ ■ ■ ■ ■ ■

Psalm 37:37,39-40

PROMISES

PROMISES

$\mathcal{W}$hat a God! His road
stretches straight and smooth.
Every GOD-direction is road-tested.
Everyone who runs toward him
Makes it.
Is there any god like GOD?

■ ■ ■ ■ ■ ■ ■ ■ ■ ■ ■ ■ ■

Psalm 18:30-31

PROMISES

$\mathscr{Y}$ou are my friends when you do the things I command you. I'm no longer calling you servants because servants don't understand what their master is thinking and planning. No, I've named you friends because I've let you in on everything I've heard from the Father.

■ ■ ■ ■ ■ ■ ■ ■ ■ ■ ■ ■ ■ ■

John 15:14-15

PROMISES

How ow exquisite your love, O God!
How eager we are to run under your wings,
To eat our fill at the banquet you spread
as you fill [us] with Eden spring water.
You're a fountain of cascading light,
and you open our eyes to light.

▪ ▪ ▪ ▪ ▪ ▪ ▪ ▪ ▪ ▪ ▪ ▪ ▪ ▪

Psalm 36:7-9

PROMISES

*T*hrough the heartfelt mercies of our God,
God's Sunrise will break in upon us,
Shining on those in the darkness,
those sitting in the shadow of death,
Then showing us the way, one foot at a time,
down the path of peace.

■ ■ ■ ■ ■ ■ ■ ■ ■ ■ ■ ■ ■ ■

Luke 1:78-79

PROMISES

Strong God...I can always count on you.
God in dependable love shows up on time....
You've been a safe place for me,
a good place to hide.
Strong God, I'm watching you do it,
I can always count on you—
God, my dependable love.

■ ■ ■ ■ ■ ■ ■ ■ ■ ■ ■ ■ ■ ■

Psalm 59:9-10,16-17

PROMISES

*T*hank you for your love,
thank you for your faithfulness;
Most holy is your name,
most holy is your Word.
The moment I called out, you stepped in;
you made my life large with strength....
Finish what you started in me, GOD.
Your love is eternal.

■ ■ ■ ■ ■ ■ ■ ■ ■ ■ ■ ■ ■ ■ ■

Psalm 138:2-3,8

PROMISES

FAITHFUL
FROM
EVERY
ANGLE

*G*OD! Let the cosmos praise your
wonderful ways,
the choir of holy angels sing anthems to
your faithful ways!...
GOD of the Angel Armies, who is like you,
powerful and faithful from every angle?

■ ■ ■ ■ ■ ■ ■ ■ ■ ■ ■ ■ ■ ■

Psalm 89:5,8

PROMISES

*H*is love has taken over our lives;
GOD's faithful ways are eternal.
Hallelujah!
Thank GOD because he's good,
because his love never quits.

Psalm 117:2; 118:1

PROMISES

*C*ultivate God-confidence.

No test or temptation that comes your way is beyond the course of what others have had to face. All you need to remember is that God will never let you down; he'll never let you be pushed past your limit; he'll always be there to help you come through it.

■ ■ ■ ■ ■ ■ ■ ■ ■ ■ ■ ■ ■ ■

1 Corinthians 10:12-13

PROMISES

$\mathcal{S}$ince God assured us, "I'll never let you
down, never walk off and leave you,"
we can boldly quote,
"God is there, ready to help;
I'm fearless no matter what.
Who or what can get to me?"

■ ■ ■ ■ ■ ■ ■ ■ ■ ■ ■ ■ ■ ■

Hebrews 13:5-6

PROMISES

I love you, GOD—
you make me strong.
GOD is bedrock under my feet,
the castle in which I live,
my rescuing knight.
My God—the high crag
where I run for dear life,
hiding behind the boulders,
safe in the granite hideout.

■ ■ ■ ■ ■ ■ ■ ■ ■ ■ ■ ■ ■ ■

Psalm 18:1-2

PROMISES

*L*ight, space, zest—that's GOD!
So, with him on my side I'm fearless,
afraid of no one and nothing.

■ ■ ■ ■ ■ ■ ■ ■ ■ ■ ■ ■

Psalm 27:1

*G*OD is all mercy and grace—
not quick to anger, is rich in love.
GOD is good to one and all;
everything he does is suffused with grace....
GOD always does what he says,
and is gracious in everything he does.

■ ■ ■ ■ ■ ■ ■ ■ ■ ■ ■ ■

Psalm 145:8-9,13

PROMISES

THE DEEPER YOUR
LOVE, THE HIGHER
IT GOES;
EVERY CLOUD IS
A FLAG TO YOUR
FAITHFULNESS.
SOAR HIGH IN THE
SKIES, O GOD!
COVER THE WHOLE
EARTH WITH YOUR
GLORY!

Psalm 57:10-11

I will put together my church, a church
so expansive with energy that not even the
gates of hell will be able to keep it out.

And that's not all. You will have complete
and free access to God's kingdom, keys to
open any and every door: no more barriers
between heaven and earth, earth and heaven.
A yes on earth is yes in heaven. A no
on earth is no in heaven.

■ ■ ■ ■ ■ ■ ■ ■ ■ ■ ■ ■ ■ ■

Matthew 16:18-19

PROMISES

Take this most seriously: A yes on earth is yes in heaven; a no on earth is no in heaven. What you say to one another is eternal. I mean this. When two of you get together on anything at all on earth and make a prayer of it, my Father in heaven goes into action. And when two or three of you are together because of me, you can be sure that I'll be there.

■ ■ ■ ■ ■ ■ ■ ■ ■ ■ ■ ■ ■

Matthew 18:18-20

PROMISES

I've already run for dear life
straight to the arms of GOD.
So why would I run away now
when you say,
"Run to the mountains; the evil
bows are bent, the wicked arrows
Aimed to shoot under cover of darkness
at every heart open to God..."?

But GOD hasn't moved to the mountains;
his holy address hasn't changed.
He's in charge, as always, his eyes
taking everything in, his eyelids
Unblinking...not missing a thing.

■ ■ ■ ■ ■ ■ ■ ■ ■ ■ ■ ■ ■ ■

Psalm 11:1-2,4

PROMISES

The person who trusts me will not only do what I'm doing but even greater things, because I, on my way to the Father, am giving you the same work to do that I've been doing. You can count on it. From now on, whatever you request along the lines of who I am and what I am doing, I'll do it. That's how the Father will be seen for who he is in the Son. I mean it. Whatever you request in this way, I'll do.

■ ■ ■ ■ ■ ■ ■ ■ ■ ■ ■ ■ ■

John 14:12-14

PROMISES

Are you sick? Call the church leaders together to pray and anoint you with oil in the name of the Master. Believing-prayer will heal you, and Jesus will put you on your feet. And if you've sinned, you'll be forgiven— healed inside and out.

Make this your common practice: Confess your sins to each other and pray for each other so that you can live together whole and healed. The prayer of a person living right with God is something powerful to be reckoned with.

■ ■ ■ ■ ■ ■ ■ ■ ■ ■ ■ ■ ■ ■

James 5:14-16

PROMISES

I look up to the mountains;
does my strength come from mountains?
No, my strength comes from GOD,
who made heaven, and earth, and mountains.
He won't let you stumble,
your Guardian God won't fall asleep....

PROMISES

GOD's your Guardian,
right at your side to protect you....
GOD guards you from every evil,
he guards your very life.
He guards you when you leave and
when you return,
he guards you now, he guards you always.

■ ■ ■ ■ ■ ■ ■ ■ ■ ■ ■ ■ ■ ■

Psalm 121:1-3,5,7-8

PROMISES

GOD
MAKES
GOOD ON
HIS WORD

*B*e good to me, God—and now!
I've run to you for dear life.
I'm hiding out under your wings....
God delivers generous love,
he makes good on his word.

■ ■ ■ ■ ■ ■ ■ ■ ■ ■ ■ ■ ■ ■

Psalm 57:1-3

PROMISES

$\mathcal{M}$y aim is to raise hopes by pointing
the way to life without end. This is the
life God promised long ago—and
he doesn't break promises!

Titus 1:2

$\mathcal{Y}$our words all add up to the sum total:
Truth.
Your righteous decisions are eternal.

Psalm 119:160

PROMISES

$\mathcal{W}$hen the Friend comes, the Spirit of the
Truth, he will take you by the hand and guide
you into all the truth there is.

■ ■ ■ ■ ■ ■ ■ ■ ■ ■ ■ ■ ■

John 16:13

PROMISES

These words I speak to you are not incidental additions to your life, homeowner improvements to your standard of living. They are foundational words, words to build a life on. If you work these words into your life, you are like a smart carpenter who built his house on solid rock. Rain poured down, the river flooded, a tornado hit—but nothing moved that house. It was fixed to the rock.

■ ■ ■ ■ ■ ■ ■ ■ ■ ■ ■ ■ ■

Matthew 7:24-25

PROMISES

I heard a voice thunder from the Throne: "Look! Look! God has moved into the neighborhood, making his home with men and women! They're his people, he's their God. He'll wipe every tear from their eyes. Death is gone for good—tears gone, crying gone, pain gone—all the first order of things gone." The Enthroned continued, "Look! I'm making everything new. Write it all down—each word dependable and accurate."

■ ■ ■ ■ ■ ■ ■ ■ ■ ■ ■ ■ ■

Revelation 21:3-5

PROMISES

For GOD's Word is solid to the core;
everything he makes is sound inside and out.
He loves it when everything fits,
when his world is in plumb-line true.
Earth is drenched
in GOD's affectionate satisfaction.

Psalm 33:4-5

PROMISES

The apostles came up and said to the Master, "Give us more faith."

But the Master said, "You don't need more faith. There is no 'more' or 'less' in faith. If you have a bare kernel of faith, say the size of a poppy seed, you could say to this sycamore tree, 'Go jump in the lake,' and it would do it."

■ ■ ■ ■ ■ ■ ■ ■ ■ ■ ■ ■ ■

Luke 17:5-6

PROMISES

The fundamental fact of existence is that this trust in God, this faith, is the firm foundation under everything that makes life worth living. It's our handle on what we can't see.

∎ ∎ ∎ ∎ ∎ ∎ ∎ ∎ ∎ ∎ ∎ ∎ ∎

Hebrews 11:1

PROMISES

He manufactures truth and justice;
All his products are guaranteed to last—
Never out-of-date, never obsolete, rust-proof.
All that he makes and does is honest and true.

■ ■ ■ ■ ■ ■ ■ ■ ■ ■ ■ ■ ■

Psalm 111:7-8

PROMISES

PROMISES

When God wanted to guarantee his promises, he gave his word, a rock-solid guarantee—God can't break his word. And because his word cannot change, the promise is likewise unchangeable.

PROMISES

We who have run for our very lives to God
have every reason to grab the promised hope
with both hands and never let go. It's an
unbreakable spiritual lifeline, reaching past all
appearances right to the very presence of God
where Jesus, running on ahead of us, has taken
up his permanent post as high priest for us.

■ ■ ■ ■ ■ ■ ■ ■ ■ ■ ■ ■ ■ ■ ■

Hebrews 6:17-20

PROMISES

The skeptic swore, "There is no God!
No God!—I can do anything I want!...
I see no evidence of a holy God.
Has anyone ever seen Anyone
climb into Heaven and take charge?
grab the winds and control them?
gather the rains in his bucket?
stake out the ends of the earth?

PROMISES

$\mathcal{J}$ust tell me his name, tell me
the names of his sons.
Come on now—tell me!"
The believer replied,
"Every promise of God proves true;
he protects everyone who runs to him for help."

■ ■ ■ ■ ■ ■ ■ ■ ■ ■ ■ ■ ■ ■

Proverbs 30:1-5

PROMISES

$\mathcal{G}$od's words are pure words,
Pure silver words refined seven times
In the fires of his word-kiln,
Pure on earth as well as in heaven.

■ ■ ■ ■ ■ ■ ■ ■ ■ ■ ■ ■ ■ ■

Psalm 12:6

PROMISES

$\mathcal{A}$ffirm your promises to me—
promises made to all who fear you....
preserve my life through your righteous ways!
Let your love, GOD, shape my life
with salvation, exactly as you promised.

■ ■ ■ ■ ■ ■ ■ ■ ■ ■ ■ ■ ■ ■

Psalm 119:38,40-41

PROMISES